Tuning In Music Book

T0385137

by the same author

Tuning In Cards
Activities in Music and Sound for Children with Complex Needs and
Visual Impairment to Foster Learning, Communication and Wellbeing
Adam Ockelford
ISBN 978 1 78592 518 4
eISBN 978 1 78450 962 0

Music, Language and Autism
Exceptional Strategies for Exceptional Minds
Adam Ockelford
ISBN 978 1 84905 197 2
eISBN 978 0 85700 428 4

First published in 2019
by Jessica Kingsley Publishers
73 Collier Street
London N1 9BE, UK
and
400 Market Street, Suite 400
Philadelphia, PA 19106, USA

www.jkp.com

Copyright © Adam Ockelford 2019
Illustrations copyright © David O'Connell 2019

Library of Congress Cataloging in Publication Data
A CIP catalog record for this book is available from the Library of Congress

British Library Cataloguing in Publication Data
A CIP catalogue record for this book is available from the British Library

ISBN 978 1 78592 517 7
eISBN 978 1 78450 955 2

Printed and bound in Great Britain

Tuning In
Music Book

Sixty-Four Songs for Children with Complex Needs and Visual Impairment to Promote Language, Social Interaction and Wider Development

Adam Ockelford

Illustrated by David O'Connell

The Amber Trust
Music for Blind Children

Jessica Kingsley *Publishers*
London and Philadelphia

With thanks to the MariaMarina Foundation whose generous support made this publication possible, and to Sally Zimmermann and Anni Martin for their specialist advice.

Introduction

The *Tuning In Music Book* is a set of 64 songs designed for children and young people who are blind or partially sighted and have learning difficulties, whether moderate, severe or profound.[1] They are suitable for the full spread of musical abilities that is to be found among this group, ranging from *Sounds of Intent* Level 1 to Level 6 (see www.soundsofintent.org). The materials represent a development and expansion of *All join in!*, which was published in the UK by the Royal National Institute of Blind People in 1996. The songs are complemented with a deck of 48 cards, the *Tuning In Cards*, which set out around 300 activities involving music and sound. These are targeted at visually impaired children and young people with complex needs, who are engaging with music at *Sounds of Intent* Levels 1 to 4.

All the resources, including recordings of the songs, are freely available in digital form on The Amber Trust website (www.ambertrust.org) for anyone to use. Those caring for or working with visually impaired children and young people with learning difficulties in the UK will also receive a free copy of this book and the cards when they are accepted on the **AmberPlus** scheme. AmberPlus provides funded termly visits from specially trained practitioners to support parents and staff at schools and centres who work with a blind or partially sighted child or young person with severe or profound learning difficulties. Parents can apply on behalf of their son or daughter by following the links on The Amber Trust website. Other copies of the *Tuning In Music Book* and *Tuning In Cards*, which are published by Jessica Kingsley Publishers, can be purchased from the usual online and retail outlets.

---

1 The *Tuning In Music Book* may also be of benefit to those without visual difficulties, including children on the autism spectrum.

How will children engage with the songs?

Children and young people will engage with the songs in different ways, depending on their level of musical development, which can be ascertained using the *Sounds of Intent* framework. This identifies six potential stages in the development of musical understanding, and three domains of engagement: **reactive** (listening and responding), **proactive** (creating or re-creating sounds and music) and **interactive** (playing or singing with others). The six levels and three domains give 18 'headlines' of musical engagement, which can be represented as shown in the diagram opposite.

At *Sounds of Intent* **Level 1**, children and young people will show no response to the songs (or, indeed, any sounds at all). However, that does not mean parents, therapists, teachers and carers should not try to engage them: it may be that a person's ability to process sound and music is still developing, or is recovering after trauma, and musical exposure and interaction may be an important feature of either of those journeys. It may also be the case that responses are occurring on a neurological level that are not apparent through clinical or functional observation.

Children and young people functioning at *Sounds of Intent* **Level 2** will experience the songs in a purely sensory way, and may join in by vocalising or making other sounds in response to what they hear. It is important to acknowledge whatever the children contribute, and to offer praise and show enthusiasm for their efforts. Be careful not to interrupt what they are doing, however. Allow plenty of time for them to process what they have heard, and remember that silence and stillness are as valid a response as any other, which may indicate concentration and enjoyment.

Children and young people at **Level 3** will be able to catch on to the simple, moment-to-moment rhythmic and melodic patterns that characterise many of the songs, and they may well try to emulate these themselves. Again, give young people time to respond. And don't be afraid of repetition, repetition, repetition: what you find tedious may be just what is required to spark a young brain into action. It is at this stage of musical development that a child may first grasp that sounds can be used symbolically – to stand for something else: an idea, a person, a place or an activity.

At **Level 4**, children and young people will start to learn, recognise and perhaps reproduce the main *motifs* from the songs: the short phrases that kick off many of the melodies, to which key words are set, and which are repeated often. In response, children may combine motifs in new ways to form 'pot pourri' songs, made up of fragments of familiar material. The motifs can also be used symbolically in their own right – with or without their accompanying words – to facilitate understanding and open up a channel of expressive communication, when language alone may not do the trick. This is generally the highest level of musical accomplishment that those with profound and multiple difficulties attain, and the strategies detailed on the *Tuning In Cards* do not move beyond this.

Level 5 is about complete songs being learnt, recognised and reproduced, at which stage children and young people may be able to join in by singing and perhaps playing melody or harmony instruments as well. It is important to remember that those with moderate or severe learning difficulties may be able to function musically as well as – or, in some cases, even better than – their 'neurotypical' peers.

At **Level 6** children and young people will be able to perform the songs persuasively for others – perhaps leading music sessions not only for friends, but for strangers too, in unfamiliar contexts; able to adapt their performance and modes of musical interaction to suit different audiences.

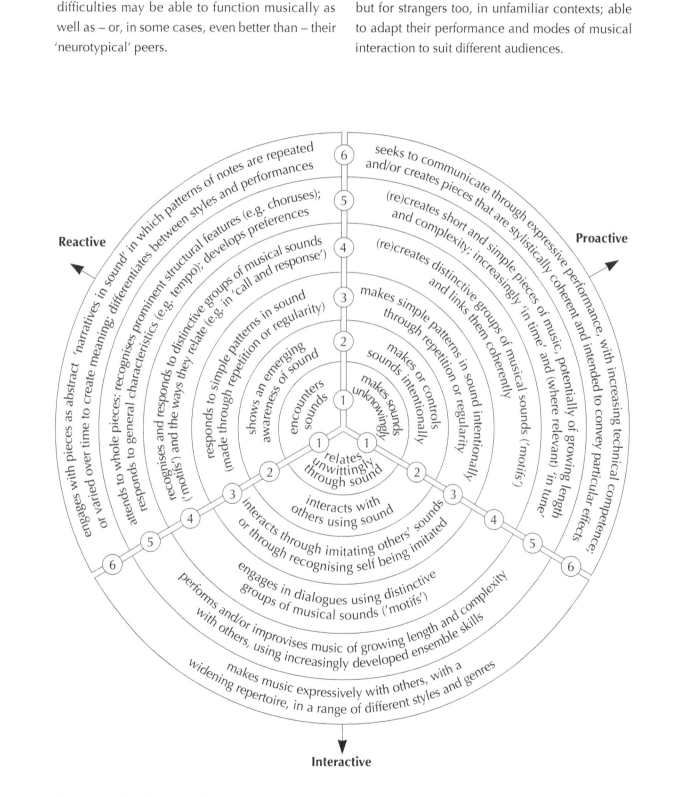

Reactive

Proactive

Interactive

**The *Sounds of Intent* framework
of musical development**

Using the materials in music sessions and beyond

The *Tuning In Music Book* songs are intended to serve two functions: as one element in a music curriculum or programme; and to promote wider learning, development and wellbeing, with a particular focus on language and communication. They can be used as the basis of formal music sessions, or in a wide range of everyday situations – at school, at home, when out and about – with or without accompaniments: **music can inform and enrich living and learning throughout the day.**

Music sessions with visually impaired children and young people with learning difficulties tend to be most effective when small numbers are involved: getting together six pupils or students and their helpers, for example, permits the feeling of belonging to a group without being overwhelmed by it. Sitting in a circle can enhance the sense of being one among others and provides the opportunity for making appropriate physical contact, which can be so important for those with little or no sight. One way of reinforcing this contact is to use equipment such as a resonance board or a giant scrunchy. The music sessions are likely to be most effective if they occur regularly and often; preferably at a set time each day. There are two sample sessions on the next page:

The songs in the *Tuning In Music Book* are designed to meet a range of needs and musical preferences. Inevitably, though, some songs will appeal to certain individuals more than others, and enjoyment is the best fuel for motivation. Whatever the level of participation, parents and carers should offer just enough support to enable children and young people to make the most of their abilities.

This support can be faded if and when the desire and capacity for independent action grows.

The idea of *choosing* is central to the *Tuning In Music Book* – its flexible structure and content enabling participants to exert control over songs, actions, people and the order in which events occur. All the songs can be augmented with communication in other modes, such as signing and using objects of reference. Whatever communication strategy is employed, it is important to remember that receptive language develops before the capacity to express thoughts and feelings. That is to say, simply *listening* is as valid a form of participation as any other – an essential developmental stage.

When singing on behalf of an individual, it will make more sense with names and pronouns, and therefore assist understanding, if only *one* person performs, effectively functioning as the voice of the youngster concerned. At other times, everyone can join in. Throughout, enthusiasm and commitment on the part of supporting adults are more important than musical precision!

Sample music session 1

For a group of six cortically blind children with profound and multiple learning difficulties, aged 5–6.

Song	Function	Time
'Music, time to sing and play'	To give the children a sense of what is about to happen	5 min
'Hello!'	To give the children a sense of who else is in the group	5 min
Nursery rhymes, with words adapted for physiotherapy	To use music to promote body awareness and movement	10 min
'All join in!' (using percussion instruments and touchscreen technology)	To give the children the opportunity to participate together and alone	5 min
'Now it's time to rest'	To encourage the children to wind down, and to signal to them that the session will soon end	2 min
'Music has finished, what shall we do next?' (using sensory cues)	To tell the children that the session is over, and to offer a transition into the next activity	3 min
	Total	**30 min**

Sample music session 2

For a group of eight young people with severe learning difficulties and visual impairment, aged 13–14.

Song	Function	Time
'Music, time to sing and play'	To prime the young people as to what is going to happen	5 min
'Who's sitting next to me?'	To let the young people know who else is in the group	5 min
'Wiggle!' (actions determined by participants)	To use music to promote body awareness and movement, choosing and taking turns	5 min
'Together and alone' (using percussion instruments and a keyboard)	To practise playing instruments, taking turns and listening to others	5 min
Listening to and then playing along with a piece of one participant's choice	To become familiar with a range of music, and to learn to share musical interests	7 min
'Can you copy me?' (using voices and instruments)	To practise musical 'call and response'	8 min
'Now it's time to rest'	To help the young people to relax, and to affirm that the session will soon be over	2 min
'Music has finished, what shall we do next?' (using objects of reference)	To signal that the session is over, and to offer a transition into the next activity	3 min
	Total	**40 min**

Concepts and language used

The concepts introduced in the songs are presented through a range of activities that children and young people who are visually impaired and have learning difficulties can experience first hand – that will therefore be of immediate relevance and potential interest to them. Although these concepts and the language through which they are expressed are suitable for those in the early stages of development, the songs are designed to be appropriate for people of *all* ages.

Everyday words and phrases are employed with the aim of promoting their understanding and use. Where possible, they are fitted into regular metrical structures and made to rhyme, and there is a good deal of repetition, all of which facilitates learning and recall.

The texts of many of the songs are meant to be customised to take into account the names of the participants or the activity chosen, and so they may vary from one occasion to another. It is even possible to make up new sets of words to fit the tunes. These may be sung unaccompanied or using the guitar or keyboard arrangements provided. Parallel versions can be produced in languages other than English if required.

The link between language and music in the songs

Throughout the *Tuning In Music Book*, music is subservient to text. The rhythm of the tunes, for example, reinforces any metrical symmetry that is used in the language, and settings largely adhere to the principle of one or two notes per syllable. Key words and phrases are consistently allocated the same rhythm and, where possible, melodic shape. This is intended to enhance verbal recognition and opens up the possibility of musical fragments acquiring symbolic meaning in their own right. For example, the melodic motifs for 'No thank you' and 'Yes please!' may come to acquire the meaning of the words, and could be used to convey the idea of 'no' and 'yes' purely through being hummed or played on an instrument.

This feature may be beneficial receptively too for children who find understanding language challenging, as their ability to handle *musical* information may nonetheless be intact. Others who have a general developmental delay may also benefit from music being used in a symbolic way, since simple musical structures, which convey a relatively small amount of auditory information, are perceptually easier to process than most spoken language, in all its richness and complexity.

No thank you   Yes please

Musical style

The songs were written primarily with ease of participation in mind. The versions available for download never move along at more than a moderate pace and each tune is limited to a range that is comfortable for most voices. The melodies are based on simple patterns of notes whose structure is easy for the ear to follow, and which are particularly suitable, therefore, for children and young people who are in the early stages of musical development (*Sounds of Intent* Levels 1–4).

The accompaniments to the songs are more sophisticated, however, introducing a wide range of instrumental colours and combinations, and couched in a variety of Western mainstream styles – 'classical', 'jazz', 'pop', 'folk', etc. The versions in this book are intended to be relatively easy to play, and include chords in addition to standard notation.

The songs and their arrangements are designed so that the most straightforward musical gesture on the part of a child or young person – vocalising or tapping a tambourine, for example – can make a fitting contribution to a potentially complex and aesthetically satisfying musical whole. However, the melodies are also suitable for unaccompanied use (in everyday situations, for instance).

It is expected that the diversity of musical styles presented in the *Tuning In Music Book* will be extended with supplementary material that reflects participants' individual preferences and cultural backgrounds.

Using the songs to promote wider learning and development, and wellbeing

As well as nurturing musical engagement, the songs in the *Tuning In Music Book* can be used to foster learning and development in other areas too, and promote wellbeing. In this respect, the materials fall into two main categories: 'Songs for language' and 'Songs for action'. There are 35 short 'Songs for language' (known as 'micro-songs'), which fall into the following groups: 'Key words and phrases', 'About me', 'My needs and wants', 'Activities', 'Other people' and 'Places'. Each song begins with a motif to which the key word or phrase is set.

These songs can be introduced during music sessions (perhaps as part of a game, or a choosing activity, which adults could initially model), but their main function is to support language and communication throughout the day. For children and young people with no expressive language, it may be best to start by introducing one or two of the 'Key words and phrases' (such as 'Yes please' and 'No thank you', or 'Hello' and 'Goodbye'). Support these musical symbols with gestures, signing, objects of reference or picture symbols. The micro-songs devised for the *Tuning In Music Book* are only intended as a starting point: try making up other songs yourself that have particular relevance to your child, and use them consistently.

There are 29 'Songs for action', that fall into one of four categories (although some of the songs can fulfil two functions or more). The songs in 'Moving to music' are based on the principle that music can provide a framework for movement (both reactively and proactively), principally through rhythm, but also through the ups and downs of the melody. The songs in 'Learning through music', take advantage of the fact music can have certain concepts associated with it, such as 'loud' and 'quiet', and 'fast' and 'slow'. The songs in 'Using music to structure other learning' provide a script for other educational and developmental activities as well as imbuing them with a sense of fun! The songs in 'Interacting with others through music' are designed to build and strengthen relationships with adults and other children, by offering a secure and predictable space within which interactions can take place. The 'Songs for action' are generally more substantial than the micro-songs designed to promote language.

Again, these songs can be introduced as part of music sessions, but can be used more widely too – in physiotherapy, for example, or as part of work in class on concepts such as cause and effect, opposites and numeracy.

Further reading

The *Tuning In Music Book* is based on many years of research. To find out more, the following books offer a starting point.

Music for Children and Young People with Complex Needs, published by Oxford University Press in 2008.

Applied Musicology: Using Zygonic Theory to Inform Music Education, Therapy, and Psychology Research, published by Oxford University Press in 2012.

Music, Language and Autism: Exceptional Strategies for Exceptional Minds, published by Jessica Kingsley Publishers in 2013.

Comparing Notes: How We Make Sense of Music, published by Profile Books in 2017.

Who do you want to see?

How are you feeling?

OTHER PEOPLE

Mum

[Teacher's name]

Dad

[Relative's name]

[Friend's name 1]

[Friend's name 2]

ABOUT ME

Happy

Sad

Not so good

Well

Angry

Tired

KEY WORDS AND PHRASES

Thank you

Yes please

No thank you

More

Hello

Finished

Goodbye

Swimming

Music

Shopping

ACTIVITIES

Watch movies

Listen to a story

What do you want to do?

Something to eat

A drink

Toilet

MY NEEDS AND WANTS

Bed

Shower

What do you want?

Class

Hall

School

Home

Outside

PLACES

Where do you want to go?

The 'micro-songs' in the *Tuning In Music Book*, which
can promote, scaffold or substitute for language

Round and round

Stretch and bend

MOVING TO MUSIC

Counting

Quiet and loud

LEARNING THROUGH MUSIC

Forwards, backwards

Wiggle

Up and down

To and fro

Sound and silence

Left, right

Fast and slow

Time to rest

Who's sitting next to me?

Find the...

All join in!

Where is the...?

What can you see?

INTERACTING WITH OTHERS THROUGH MUSIC

What is it?

USING MUSIC TO STRUCTURE OTHER LEARNING

In the circle

Can you copy me?

What are we having for lunch?

Can you find your...?

Together and alone

Listen!

What day is it?

The 'songs for action' in the
Tuning In Music Book

15

Key words and phrases
motif map

p. 18

Hel – lo

p. 17

Yes please

p. 17

No thank you

p. 17

More, more, I'd like some more

p. 17

Thank you

p. 19

Fin – ished

p. 19

Good-bye

Key words and phrases

Yes please

Yes please, Yes please, Yes please.

No thank you

No thank you, no thank you, no thank you ve-ry much!

Thank you

Thank you, thank you, thank you ve-ry much in-deed.

More

More, more, I'd like some more.

Hello

18

Goodbye

Finished

About me
motif map

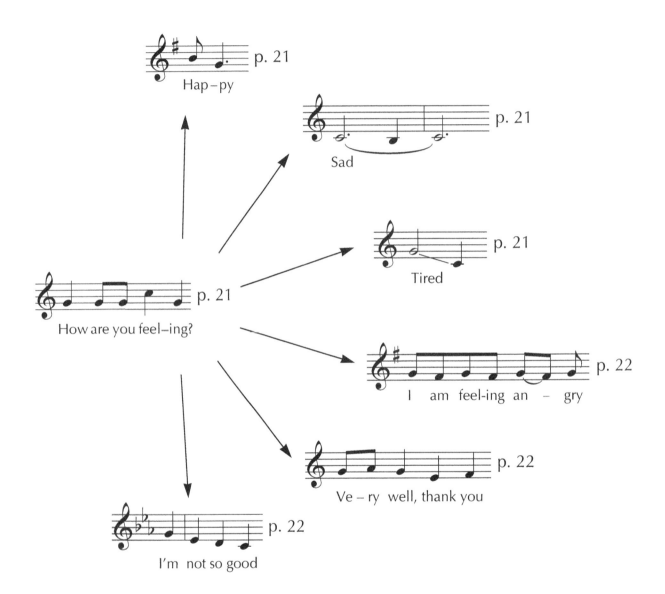

About me

I am feeling angry

Very well thank you

I'm not so good

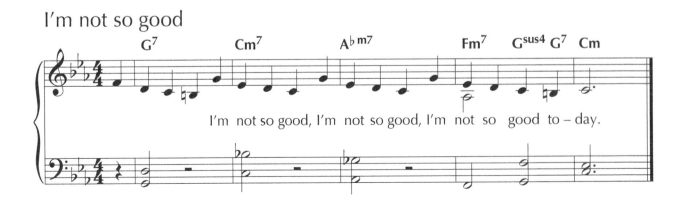

My needs and wants
motif map

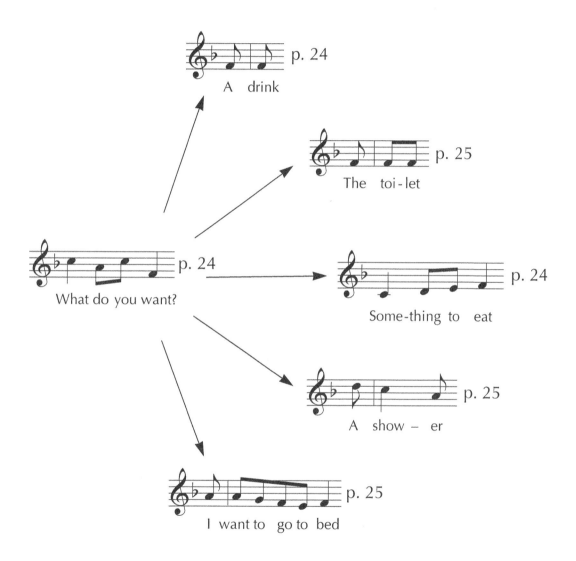

My needs and wants

What do you want?

What do you want? What do you want? Tell me what it is.

A drink

A drink, a drink, I would like a drink, please!

Something to eat

Some-thing to eat, Some-thing to eat,

I'd like some – thing to eat, please.

Toilet

The toi-let,   the toi-let,   I need the toi-let.

Bed

I want to go to bed, I want to go to bed, I'm tired and I want to go to bed.

Shower

A show – er, a show – er, I'd like to take a show – er. A

show – er, a show – er, I'd like to take a show – er.

Activities
motif map

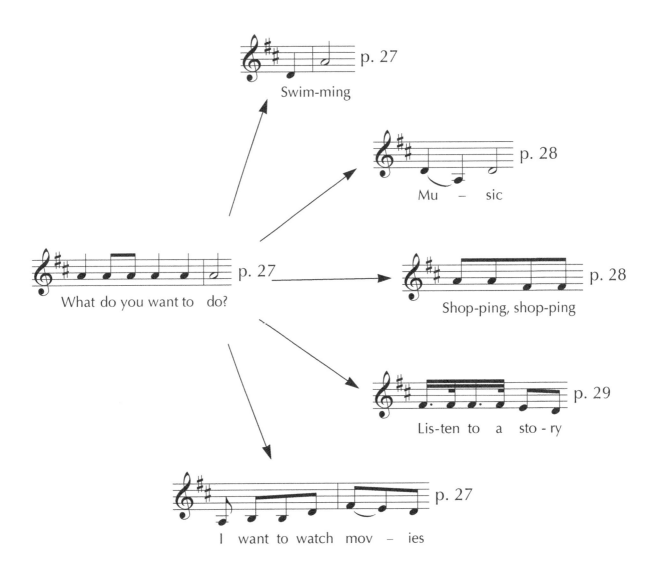

Swim-ming — p. 27

Mu – sic — p. 28

What do you want to do? — p. 27

Shop-ping, shop-ping — p. 28

Lis-ten to a sto-ry — p. 29

I want to watch mov – ies — p. 27

Activities

What do you want to do?

Note: A

Chord: A^sus2

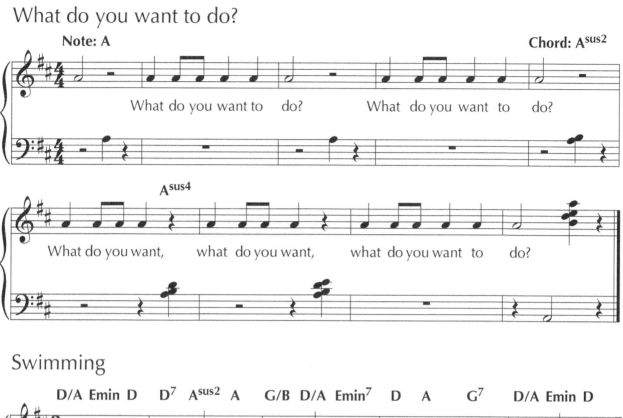

What do you want to do? What do you want to do?

A^sus4

What do you want, what do you want, what do you want to do?

Swimming

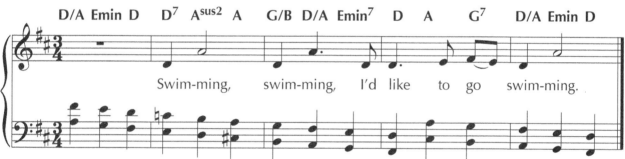

D/A Emin D D^7 A^sus2 A G/B D/A Emin^7 D A G^7 D/A Emin D

Swim-ming, swim-ming, I'd like to go swim-ming.

Watch movies

D D/C♯

I want to watch mov – ies, mov – ies,

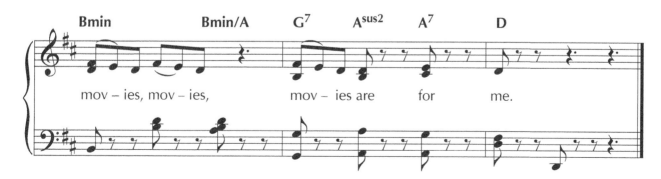

Bmin Bmin/A G^7 A^sus2 A^7 D

mov – ies, mov – ies, mov – ies are for me.

Shopping

Shop-ping, shop-ping,
Shop-ping, shop-ping,
Shop-ping is what I want to do!

Music

Mu - sic,
time.
time to sing and
Sing and play, a - long,
play.

come and join
us.
Come and join us in the cir - cle

now.
In the cir - cle, now it's mu - sic time.

Listen to a story

Other people
motif map

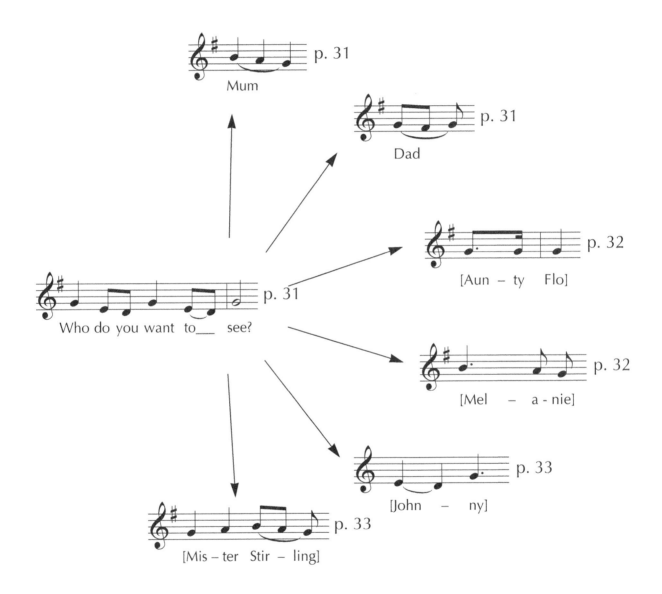

Other people

Who do you want to see?

Who do you want to see?

Tell me who it 'll be. Tell me who,

tell me who, tell me who it 'll be.

Mum

Mum, Mum, I'd like to see my Mum.

Dad

Dad, Dad, I'd like to see my Dad.

Relative

Friend

Friend

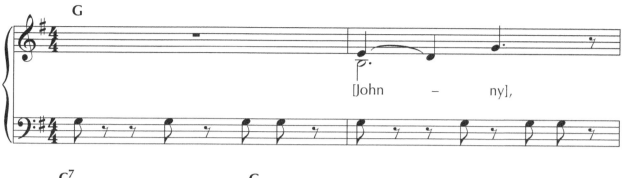

[John – ny],

[John – ny], I'd like to see [John – ny]

Teacher

[Mis – ter Stir – ling],

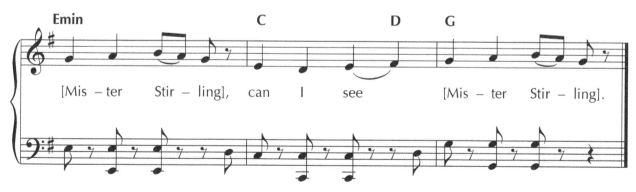

[Mis – ter Stir – ling], can I see [Mis – ter Stir – ling].

Places
motif map

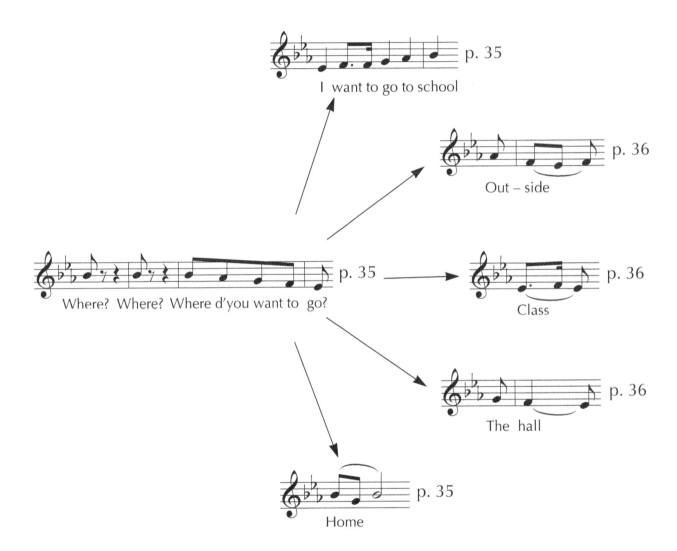

Places

Where do you want to go?

Where? Where? Where d'you want to go?

Home

Home, home, time to go home.

School

I want to go to school, I want to go to school.

Class

Class, class, I'd like to go to class.

Hall

The hall, the hall, I'd like to go to the hall.

Outside

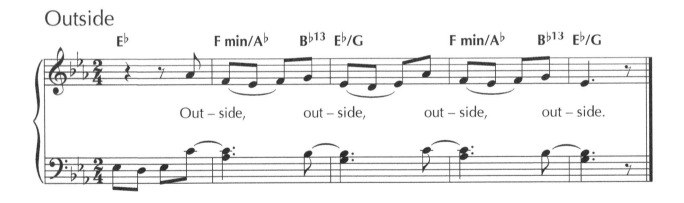

Out – side, out – side, out – side, out – side.

Moving to music
song map

Stretch and bend

Stretch your [arms]   p. 39

Left, right

Left,   right   p. 43

Up and down

Go - ing up   and down   p. 42

Wiggle

[Wig   –   gle] your [toes],   pp. 44–45

Round and round

Round and round   p. 38

Forwards, backwards

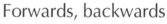

For-wards, back-wards   p. 46

To and fro

We're [rock – ing]   pp. 40–41

Time to rest

Now it's time to   rest   p. 47

Round and round

Aim: to provide a musical scaffolding for turning movements.

This song can accompany rotation of the hands, wrists, arms, legs, feet or head – or the whole body – rolling or dancing, for example. Props (a decorated stick, a shaker, a pom-pom, wrist or ankle bells) can be used to add an extra multisensory dimension, and to increase the physicality of the task.

Stretch and bend

Aim: to encourage movement and body awareness through music.

This song can be used within music sessions or to support physiotherapy as an activity in its own right. The stretching and bending may involve arms, legs or fingers. The movements may be undertaken coactively with adult helpers, or children and young people may work in pairs if they are able to. Props may be used, such as a large scrunchy or wrist or ankle bells, to add additional sensory input.

To and fro

Aim: to provide music to stimulate and accompany smooth rocking and swaying movements.

This song provides a regular rhythmic scaffold for rocking and swaying movements. Children and young people can engage coactively with adults, or could potentially be supported to work in pairs. Activities could involve gross motor and balance apparatus.

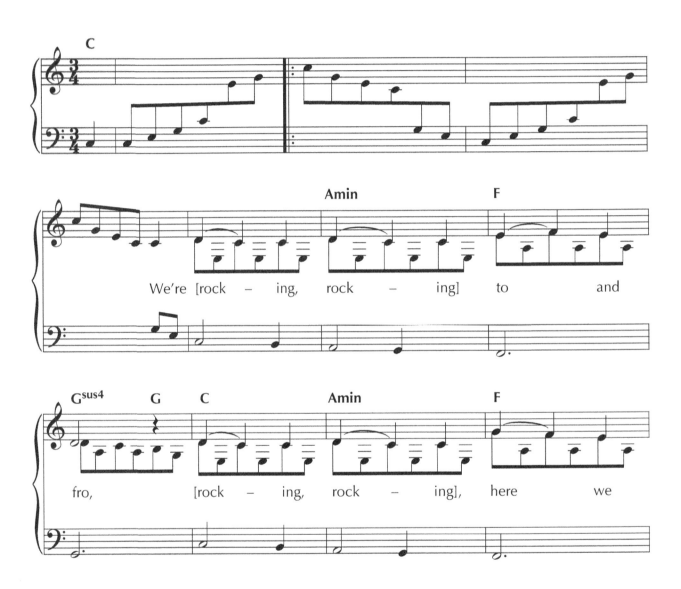

We're [rock – ing, rock – ing] to and fro, [rock – ing, rock – ing], here we

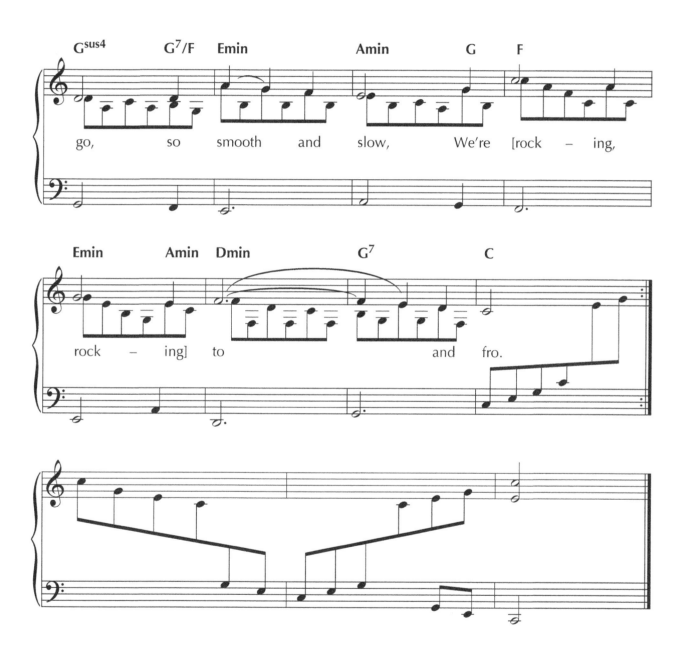

Up and down

Aim: to provide a musical representation of up and down movements.

This song can be used to encourage children to move their arms, legs or head. Indicate to them first (perhaps using touch as well as other forms of communication) which part of the body it is to be. Children and young people may be able to choose which part of their body they wish to move up and down next. The effect can be enhanced by raising something bright or rustly. The movements can be made with any degree of support that is necessary. For visually impaired children, songs such as this are particularly important in that they provide an auditory representation of movement.

42

Left and right

Aim: to promote the understanding of left and right.

The idea of left and right can be enhanced by moving or touching the appropriate arm, elbow, hand, leg, knee, foot, ear or eye. Different soundmakers can be used consistently to reinforce the concept – for example, bells on the right wrist and a rattle in the left hand.

Wiggle

Aim: to provide a musical framework for shaking movements and others similar.

This song can accompany shaking, wiggling or flapping of hands, toes, the head, and so on. Something can be shaken that is glittery or rattles – providing additional visual or auditory stimulation.

[wig — gle] your, [wig — gle] your [toes].

[toes].

Forwards, backwards

Aim: to encourage back and forth movement and an understanding of the associated concepts.

This back and forth movement can be done in a number of ways: sitting opposite a partner, for example, or in a wheelchair. The sense of changing direction can be enhanced with a sound in front of the child or young person and one behind. The song can be sung at different speeds to suit the physical attributes of different participants.

Time to rest

Aim: to promote relaxation through listening to music.

This song can be used in conjunction with other relaxation techniques. When used as part of a formal music session, the song may be used consistently to introduce other relaxing music, and to indicate that the session will be ending shortly.

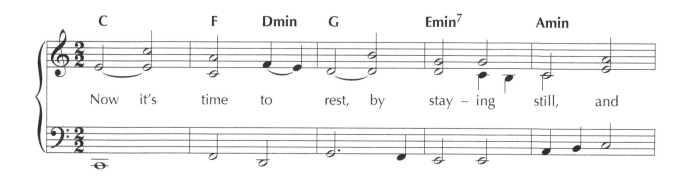

Learning through music
song map

Sound and silence

You're play-ing with the mus-ic

pp. 50–51

Slowly and quickly

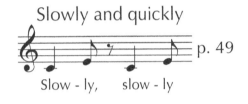

Slow - ly,   slow - ly

p. 49

Quiet and loud

Play ve-ry quiet-ly,

p. 54

Counting

One, two, three, four, five.

pp. 52–53

Slowly and quickly

Aim: to give the experience and promote the understanding of slow and fast.

This song can be used as a group or individual activity. Different soundmakers can be used, including gesture and beam technologies, potentially involving a range of different types of movement.

Sound and silence

Aim: to help the understanding of sound and its absence – of playing or *not* playing.

This song can be used with the group playing together or with children and young people on their own. Any soundmakers can be used. The pauses can be held for increasing lengths of time, as participants' capacity to anticipate what is coming next grows.

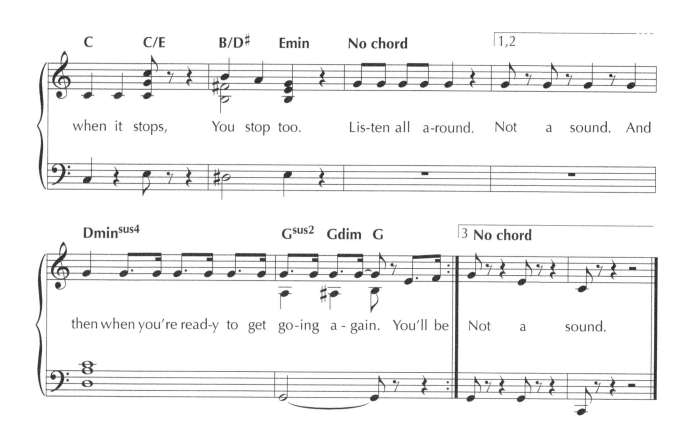

Counting

Aim: to provide a motivating context to practise counting from one to five and back.

This song can be taken at different speeds – as slowly as required at first for children and young people to be able to participate reactively or proactively. Begin by numbering fingers. For those who are unable to see, each finger can be given a squeeze and a wiggle to enhance its identity, and helping children to anticipate which will be next. Later, it may be possible to count objects.

Quiet and loud

Aim: to promote the understanding of quiet and loud and to experience making quiet and loud sounds.

Vocalising and singing may be involved as well as instruments or other soundmakers. Children and young people may make contrasting movements: tapping gently with their toes and then stamping their feet, for example.

Using music to structure other learning
song map

What day is it today?

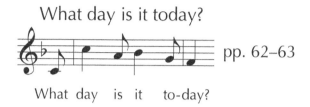

pp. 62–63

What day is it to-day?

What's for lunch?

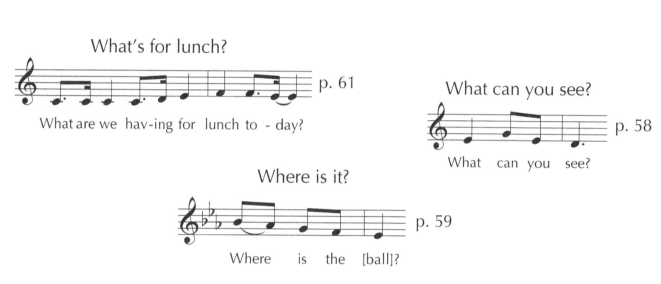

p. 61

What are we hav-ing for lunch to - day?

What can you see?

p. 58

What can you see?

Where is it?

p. 59

Where is the [ball]?

What is it?

p. 57

What is it?

Can you find your ...?

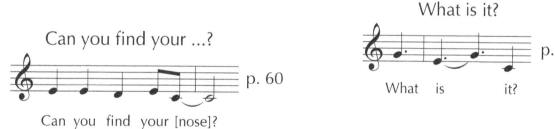

p. 60

Can you find your [nose]?

Finding and giving

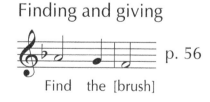

p. 56

Find the [brush]

Finding and giving

Aim: to provide a musical framework for encouraging children and young people to find things and hand them to someone else.

Sing the song first and then do the action, or keep repeating the song as required. Use everyday objects. Only one object need be available at first or the choice may be limited to two or more things as appropriate. Give support as necessary to achieve the task. It may be possible to facilitate children working in pairs.

Find the [brush] and give it to me. Thank you ve – ry much in-deed

What is it?

Aim: to provide a musical framework within which objects are recognised and named.

Have a small selection of objects ready (just two – or even a single item – to start with). A helper may answer on behalf of the child or young person, or alternative forms of communication may be used.

What can you see?

Aim: to provide a musical framework within which objects are seen and named.

Have a picture or object ready to be viewed and (if possible) named. A teacher, carer or parent may answer on behalf of the child or young person.

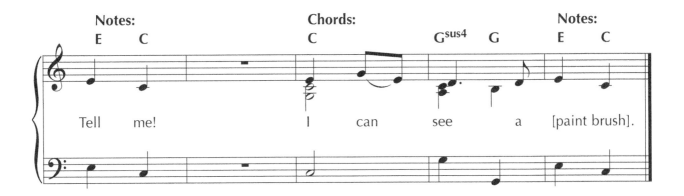

Where is it?

Aim: to provide a musical framework within which the locations of things can be identified and that information can be shared with others.

Have an object ready to be noticed (or found by touch). Subsequently, try using two objects or more.

Where is the [ball]? Can you show me where it

is? Here's the [ball]. Here it is.

Can you find your...?

Aim: to provide a musical framework for encouraging children and young people to become more aware of themselves and their bodies.

Offer physical prompts at the appropriate level for the child or young person concerned. Be particularly sensitive with those with no sight at all, who may find it difficult to anticipate what is coming next.

What's for lunch?

Aim: to provide a musical framework for encouraging children and young people to anticipate what they will be having to eat at their next meal.

Initially, the song can be used at lunch time with an item of food present in front of the child. Subsequently, it may be possible to use the song to anticipate what there will be to eat (from a selection of two possibilities or more).

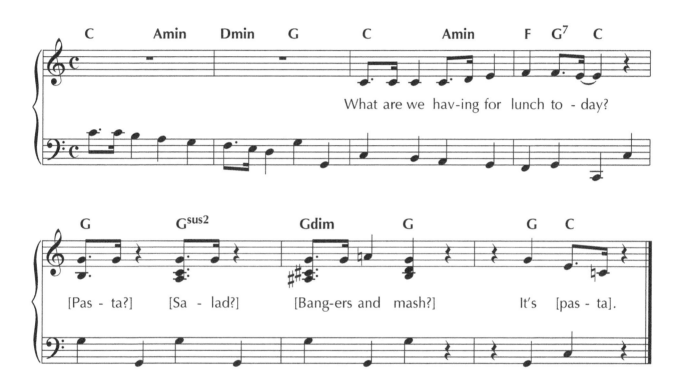

What day is it today?

Aim: to reinforce the concept of days of the week – their sequence and which day it is today.

This song can be used in conjunction with special signs, objects of reference, activities or even fragrances that characterise the day. The song can lead to a consideration of what is to happen today (or this morning or this afternoon) using, where appropriate, signs, an object timetable, or songs to indicate particular activities.

Interacting with others through music

song map

Who's sitting next to me?

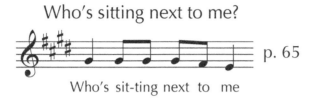

p. 65

Who's sit-ting next to me

All join in!

p. 68

[Clap your hands]

In the circle

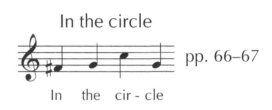

pp. 66–67

In the cir - cle

Can you copy me?

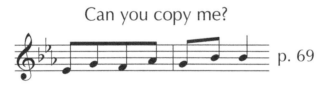

p. 69

Can you make the sound I make?

Listen!

p. 72

Lis - ten!

Together and alone

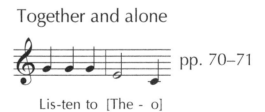

pp. 70–71

Lis-ten to [The - o]

Who's sitting next to me?

Aim: to provide a musical framework for greeting, giving the opportunity to touch or shake hands; to foster awareness of the group and of everyone's position within it.

This singing moves round a circle of participants, from the left or the right (it is good to be consistent from day to day). Children and young people reinforce the musical greeting with physical contact, by touching or shaking hands. In songs such as this, where helpers may be singing on behalf of individuals, participants' feeling of identity may be enhanced if only *one* person performs on their behalf. The concept of individuality may be further strengthened by using personal soundmakers.

In the circle

Aim: to use the structure of a song to scaffold social engagement – taking turns, copying, listening to others and making a contribution.

The sound that is conveyed from one participant to another could be a vocalisation, made by a traditional instrument, or controlled using beam or gesture technology. Teachers, carers and parents can offer whatever level of support is needed to ensure the social interactions take place.

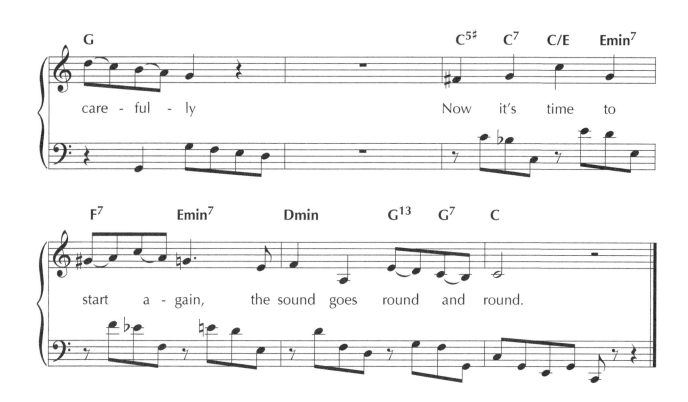

All join in!

Aim: to provide a simple musical structure suitable for accompanying a wide range of sound-making and other actions.

Possibilities include clapping hands, slapping knees, stamping feet, scratching head, tickling tummy, touching the ground, tapping the chair, banging the drum, shaking the shaker, and making sounds using gesture or beam technology. Children and young people can make the sounds and do the actions individually or as a group, or the group can copy what an individual decides to do.

Can you copy me?

Aim: to promote the understanding of copying in sound; to provide a musical framework for utilising this knowledge.

This song is intended to be sung first to introduce a copying activity. Any sounds can be used, including body-sounds, vocalising, and sounds made with instruments or everyday soundmakers. To begin with, helpers can copy participants, or one member of staff can copy another on behalf of a pupil or student. This modelling of the activity may assist in children's developing the concept of imitation.

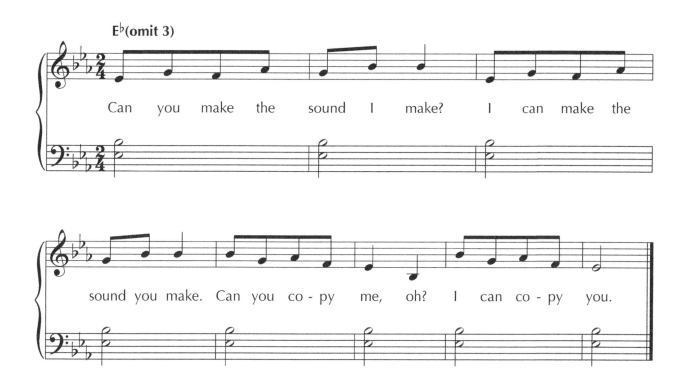

Together and alone

Aim: to provide a musical framework for introducing the idea of doing something on your own, listening to others, and playing with the group.

A wide range of everyday soundmakers and instruments can be used, and children and young people may join in using switches or other assistive technology. This is an activity that can be done in a relatively large group.

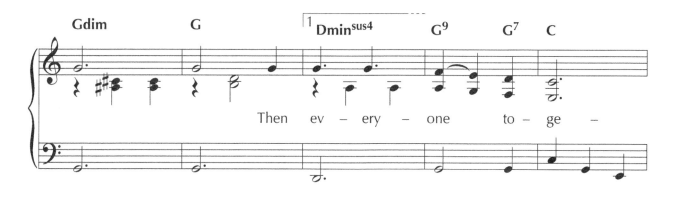

Then ev – ery – one to – ge –

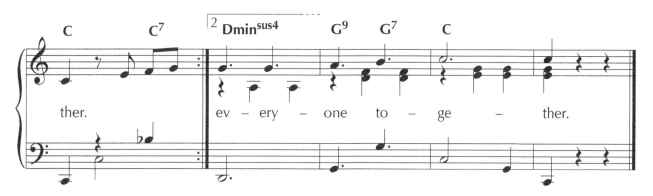

ther.   ev – ery – one to – ge – ther.

Listen!

Aim: to provide a musical framework for taking turns, listening to others, making sounds and playing instruments.

Any instrument can be used: a drum, scraper, bells, tambourine, shaker, claves and so on. Other sounds may be accessed through switches, or movement or gesture technology. Everyday soundmakers can also be used. Where appropriate, participants can be asked to choose the instrument that they would like to play. The group can play together.